Learn My Language! Spanish

Spanish Words in the House

By Robert Kennedy

Gareth Stevens Publishing

Please visit our website, www.garethstevens.com. For a free color catalog of all our high-quality books, call toll free 1-800-542-2595 or fax 1-877-542-2596.

Library of Congress Cataloging-in-Publication Data

Kennedy, Robert.
Spanish words in the house / by Robert Kennedy.
 p. cm. — (Learn my language! Spanish)
Includes index.
ISBN 978-1-4824-0363-3 (pbk.)
 ISBN 978-1-4824-0364-0 (6-pack)
ISBN 978-1-4824-0360-2 (library binding)
1. Dwellings — Juvenile literature. 2. Spanish language — Vocabulary — Juvenile literature. I. Title.
TH4811.5 K46 2014
468—dc23

First Edition

Published in 2014 by
Gareth Stevens Publishing
111 East 14th Street, Suite 349
New York, NY 10003

Copyright © 2014 Gareth Stevens Publishing

Designer: Sarah Liddell
Editor: Therese Shea

Photo credits: Cover, p. 1 Breadmaker/Shutterstock.com; pp. 5, 21 Monkey Business Images/Shutterstock.com; p. 7 Dominik Pabis/E+/Getty Images; pp. 9, 11, 17 Artazum/Shutterstock.com; p. 13 zstock/Shutterstock.com; p. 15 iStockphoto/Thinkstock.com; p. 19 Lisa Romerein/FoodPix/Getty Images.

All rights reserved. No part of this book may be reproduced in any form without permission in writing from the publisher, except by a reviewer.

Printed in the United States of America

CPSIA compliance information: Batch #CW14GS: For further information contact Gareth Stevens, New York, New York at 1-800-542-2595.

Contents

My *Casa* 4

The Party 6

The Living Room 8

My Bedroom 10

The Kitchen 12

The Yard 14

The Bathroom 16

At the Table 18

Hasta la Vista 20

Glossary 22

For More Information 23

Index 24

Boldface words appear in the glossary.

My *Casa*

My family often speaks *español*. That's the Spanish word for Spanish. Would you like to learn? Come to my house! The Spanish word for house is *casa*.

Spanish = español (ehs-pah-NYOHL)

house = casa (KAH-sah)

The Party

I'm glad you're here. It's a special day. We're having a party, or *fiesta*. We got balloons for the party. The Spanish word for balloons is *globos*.

party = fiesta (FYEHS-tah)

balloons = globos (GLOH-bohs)

The Living Room

First, I'll show you around. This is the living room. The Spanish word for living room is *salón*. Have a seat in my *silla*. That's Spanish for chair.

living room = salón (sah-LOHN)

chair = silla (SEE-yah)

My Bedroom

This is my bedroom. The Spanish word for bedroom is *habitación*. That's my bed, or *cama*. It's very **comfortable**! I read on my *cama*, too.

bedroom = habitación (ah-bee-tah-SYOHN)

bed = cama (KAH-mah)

The Kitchen

Let's grab a **snack** in the *cocina*. That's Spanish for kitchen. I look in the refrigerator, or *refrigerador*. There's lots of food in there!

kitchen = cocina (Koh-SEE-nah)

refrigerator = refrigerador (rreh-free-heh-rah-DOHR)

The Yard

Let's go in the yard and play now. The Spanish word for backyard is *patio*. We can play catch with my dog, or *perro*. He loves to run!

yard = patio (PAH-tyoh)

dog = perro (PEH-rroh)

The Bathroom

My hands got very dirty outside. It's time to wash up. Here's the *baño*. That's Spanish for bathroom. I wash my hands at the sink, or *lavamanos*.

bathroom = baño (BAH-nyoh)

sink = lavamanos (lah-vah-MAH-nohs)

lavamanos

At the Table

It's time for the party! We sit down at the *mesa*. That's the Spanish word for table. I put lots of food on my plate, or *plato*. How many **tamales** would you like on your *plato*?

table = mesa (MEH-sah)

plate = plato (PLAH-toh)

Hasta la Vista

Do you live in a house or *apartamento*? That's Spanish for apartment. Can I come and visit you there? ¡*Hasta la vista!* That means "see you soon!"

apartment = apartamento
(ah-par-tah-MEHN-toh)

see you soon = hasta la vista
(AHS-tah lah VEES-tah)

Glossary

comfortable: restful and relaxing

snack: a small meal or amount of food

tamale: a Mexican dish of chopped meat and peppers surrounded with cornmeal and wrapped in a corn husk

For More Information

Books

Gordon, Sharon. *At Home in the City = Mi Casa en la Ciudad.* New York, NY: Marshall Cavendish Benchmark, 2007.

Medina, Sarah. *Spanish.* Chicago, IL: Heinemann Library, 2012.

Petelinsek, Kathleen, and E. Russell Primm. *Home = Casa.* Chanhassen, MN: Child's World, 2005.

Websites

Spanish Around the Home
spanish.about.com/od/wordlists/a/house.htm
Check this list to learn more Spanish words for objects and rooms around your home.

Spanish House
www.spanishlanguageguide.com/vocabulary/house.asp
Read more Spanish vocabulary and learn how to say sentences, too.

Publisher's note to educators and parents: Our editors have carefully reviewed these websites to ensure that they are suitable for students. Many websites change frequently, however, and we cannot guarantee that a site's future contents will continue to meet our high standards of quality and educational value. Be advised that students should be closely supervised whenever they access the Internet.

Index

apartment/
 apartamento 20
backyard/patio 14
balloons/globos 6, 7
bathroom/baño 16
bed/cama 10, 11
bedroom/habitación 10
chair/silla 8, 9
dog/perro 14, 15
house/casa 4, 5
kitchen/cocina 12
living room/salón 8
party/fiesta 6
plate/plato 18, 19
refrigerator/
 refrigerador 12, 13
see you soon/hasta la vista 20
sink/lavamanos 16, 17
Spanish/español 4
table/mesa 18, 19